Publishing Director: Jean-Paul Manzo

Text: Klaus H. Carl

Publishing assistant: Vanessa Basille

Design, cover and jacket: Cédric Pontes

Layout: Matthieu Carré

© Parkstone Press Ltd, New York, USA, 2002
ISBN 1 85995 850 8
Printed and bound in Hong Kong

© Klaus H.Carl: ill.5, 6, 9, 10, 13, 19, 21, 23, 24, 25, 33, 34, 38, 39, 41, 42, 43, 44, 45, 46, 47, 48, 49, 50, 51, 52, 54, 55, 57, 58, 59, 60, 61, 63, 64, 65, 68, 69, 70, 71, 75, 80, 83, 87, 88, 92, 94, 95, 96, 98, 99, 100, 101, 104, 105, 106, 107, 108, 109, 110, 111, 113.

© Roni Sofer: ill. 1, 15, 16, 37, 66, 67, 72, 73, 76, 81, 82, 84, 85, 103.

© Sabine Reuss: ill. 3, 62, 74, 77, 90, 91, 93, 102, 112.

© Office du tourisme de Grèce/Frankfurt: ill. 17, 18, 22,27, 29, 30, 31, 40, 53, 56, 97.

© Pictures Colour Library: ill.14, 20, 78, 79.

© Archeological Receipts Fund: ill. 84, 86.

Athens

Klaus H. Carl

1. General view of Athens.

Introduction......6
Of Gods and Men......9

History......12
The Trojan War......14
Forms of government in Athens......16
Four centuries BC and after......16

Temples and Theatres......22

Tour of the city......30
The Acropolis......30
Two Theatres......37
The Areiopagos......40
The Greek Agora......43
The Roman Agora......45
The Tower of the Winds......46
The Hadrian Library......49
The Olympeion......52
The Olympic stadium......52
The Plaka......54
The Cathedral and Churches......65
The Kerameikos cemetery......67
The Lykabettos......71
The centre......72
The Museums......85
Piraeus......88

Epilogue......91

Greek Gods......92

Annexes......94

Introduction

Athens – the very name evokes the memory of ancient legends; it represents to us the pinnacle of classical tragedy, the birthplace of western culture, and the very first Olympic games. It is a name known throughout the world. And yet despite the fact that the city, which currently boasts a population of around 5 million and covers an area of almost 430 square kilometres, is fast growing to a size you could compare with other European capitals such as Rome, Lisbon or Berlin, not many people could really claim to know modern Athens, one of Europe's oldest capitals.

The city of Athens lies on the Attic peninsula next to the Gulf of Saronikos, in a broad valley flanked on three sides by mountains, some of which are over 1,000 metres high. On the fourth side, to the west, stand the Agaleos hills. Like many Greek cities, the Polis was originally built on a hill. This formed the original town centre and was later extended into a fortress. As time passed, the city spread beyond the hill and reached the Pnyx and Lykabettos hills as well. These two hills now stand right in the centre of the city, where they dominate the sprawl of surrounding houses. On several occasions ancient Athens was conquered by its foes, leaving only a few houses standing. Its subsequent reconstruction, which gave the city its present-day form, did not take place until the 19th century, after Athens was made capital of Greece in 1834. Today, thanks to its university, its many museums and archaeological sites, the city is once again the intellectual centre of Greece. It has close links with the harbour town of Piraeus, located only six kilometres away. Piraeus is the country's main port, served not only by island ferries, but also by large cargo ships, and, of course, calling cruise liners.

Greece is situated on the southeastern edge of Europe. It is bordered in the north by several Balkan countries, in the west and south by the Mediterranean, and in the east by the Aegean. Its mountainous countryside covers an area of around 130,000 km². The highest of its mountains is Olympus – home of the gods, according to the ancient Greeks – which is approximately 2,900 metres in height. Its many peninsulas, islands and groups of islands - the Cyclades, Sporades, Crete, Mykonos and Rhodes - are the favourite holiday destinations of thousands of tourists who descend each summer on their peaceful shores.

2. Alvise Gramolin, *Aegean Sea*, 1642, 1070 x 650 cm. Bibliothèque Nationale, Paris.

3. View of Athens and the Lykabettos hill, from the Acropolis.

4. Drawing of Greek gods.

5. Daedalus and Icarus, relief,
   Byzantine Museum, Athens.

In terms of religious faith, the 10-million strong population of Greece belongs almost entirely to the Greek Orthodox Church. Their language is the oldest in Europe, and for that reason alone is a symbol of the country's historical continuity. Modern Greek may sound different, but in reality it is only a few steps removed from the language in which Homer penned his *Iliad* and *Odyssey*. So, its influence on European culture has been a long and constant one.

Greek mythology is still vividly alive today among the ruins of the Acropolis and the Parthenon, and in the lanes and shady squares of Athens' old town. Here, one is reminded of the pantheon of Greek gods and goddesses – the bitterly feuding divine couple Zeus and Hera, brave Athena, or winged Hermes, the messenger of the gods. How easy it is to imagine the heroes of Homer's epics treading these paths - wily Odysseus, bloodthirsty Achilles, or mighty Hector. With every step one takes across the city, we are met by the familiar faces of ancient mythology. There is Daedalus and Icarus, who made wings for themselves from wax and feathers to try to escape the labyrinth of Minos and the fearsome Minotaur, or Sisyphus, who was punished for his duplicity by being given the eternal task of pushing a rock up a hill that would roll down again as soon as he reached the top. Mythical events as well as historical ones such as the Peloponnesian War or the numerous battles of the Greeks against the Persians or Turks have left their mark on the city. Athens was also the cradle of democracy: Aristotle first invented the idea of a democratic constitution, designed as a third form of state alongside monarchy and oligarchy, and it was Pericles who first applied democracy – albeit in a very conservative form – in practice.

Greek culture has had a huge impact on European intellectual life over the centuries. Around the 5th century BC, Aristophanes first used a dramatic form known as comedy, and it is thanks to the works of Sophocles and Euripides that we have tragedy. It was Greek thinkers such as Socrates and Anaxagoras who developed the concept of philosophy that was to influence Western thoughts for centuries to come. The first ancient Olympic Games were held in Athens in 776 BC, as were the first modern ones (in 1896), while the first games of the third millennium will also be held here in 2004.

Of Gods and Men

Just like other cultures, the Greeks tried to understand and explain the origins of the world. For them, its origin was attributed to Chaos, from which came Gaia, the earth. Gaia gave birth to the mysterious Tartarus, and to Hades, god of the underworld, Uranus, god of the heavens and Pontos, god of the sea. From the darkness came light, and the earth created from itself not only the skies which surround it, but also its mountains and seas. Greek mythology tells of giants with 100 arms, of Cyclops and power-hungry Titans, the product of the union of Gaia and her son Uranus.

6. *Poseidon*, marble statue,
 found at Melos,
 Archaeological Museum,
 Athens.

7. Noël Nicolas Coypel, *Birth of
 Venus (Aphrodite)*, 1732,
 Oil on canvas, 81 x 65 cm.
 Hermitage Museum,
 St Petersburg.

Uranus kept his children in a dark dungeon, and in revenge for this cruelty his son Chronos, youngest of the Titans and the god of time, castrated his father with a sickle. Uranus' manhood, thus taken from him, was used to make the sea fertile, and from its surf arose the goddess of love, Aphrodite. From the drops of blood which fell on the earth during Chronos' wrath came the Furies and giants who threatened the gods. Chronos, who ruled over his brothers, finally married his sister Rhea. It was prophesied that one of his sons would become his successor, and so Chronos ate his children as soon as they were born. Chronos, just like his father Uranus, kept the giants and Cyclops to guard him in Tartarus.

Rhea was not prepared to put up with the cruelties of her husband and managed to save her newborn son Zeus. When Chronos came home on the night after Zeus' birth, intending to eat this child as well, Rhea tricked her heartless husband by giving him a stone wrapped up in swaddling clothes instead of the child. She had the baby taken to Crete, where he grew up under the protection of trusted friends.

When he was older, Zeus forced his father to bring his brothers and sisters back to life, and thus Hestia, Demeter, Hera, Hades and Poseidon were reborn. Together, they declared war on Chronos and the Titans. They eventually gained control over the giants and Cyclops and freed them from Tartarus.

The war of the gods finally ended after a long and bloody struggle. Power was divided between Chronos' three victorious sons: Zeus was to rule the heavens, Poseidon the sea, and Hades the underworld.

However, their power, particularly Zeus', did not remain unchallenged and there followed several battles against colossal monsters that forced him again and again to use his fiercest weapon - the lightning bolt. Until then, there were no mortals among the ancient gods. It was Prometheus – he and his brothers Atlas, Menoitius and Epimetheus, descended from the Titan Japetus - who created them out of clay. However, Zeus so hated this family that he threw Japetus and the other Titans into Tartarus. He then slew the mighty Menoitius with a lightning bolt, made Atlas bear the whole weight of the heavens on his shoulders, and finally made Epimetheus bring misfortune upon the human race. Zeus welded Prometheus, who had betrayed the gods by bringing the knowledge of fire to mortals, to a rock. To increase his torment, each day at noon a vulture pecked at his liver – thought by the Greeks to be the seat of one's desires - which renewed itself immediately afterwards. Zeus' son Heracles, together with Alcmene, freed Prometheus from his punishment only after Zeus finally gave his permission for them to do so.

In the meantime, Epimetheus, despite repeated warnings from Prometheus, married Pandora, mistress of all womanly wiles. She managed to open her husband's box, in which he kept both good and bad things, and it poured misfortune onto earth and on all mankind. In dismay, she immediately shut the box, only to seal hope once again inside.

To add to this misfortune, Zeus created a great flood, from which only two people survived: Deukalion, son of Prometheus, and Pyrrha, daughter of Epimetheus, who finally settled on Mount Parnassus. A mysterious voice ordered them to throw the bones of their mother behind them. They followed this strange request and threw stones that had been lying in the fields onto the earth. From those stones grew a new human race.

8. Drawing of the god Apollo.

9. Statue of Zeus, Archaeological Museum, Athens.

History

We know about Greek history principally from the two historians: Herodotus (484-425 BC) and Thucydides (c. 460-395 BC). Their history begins approximately with the Bronze Age, around the middle of the 3rd millennium BC. The first signs of settlement around the Acropolis date back to around this time. In Attica, which was a fraction of the size of today's Athens, kings ruled over people who lived in modest huts. Traditionally, the mythical-historical figure of King Cecrops is mentioned, also known as "the autochthonous" (born of the earth) and as the founder of Athens. He was represented, because of his introduction of monogamy, by a double face, one male, and one female. He divided Attica into 12 tribal areas, introduced the Areiopagos, or law court, and arbitrated in the dispute concerning the name of the city between Athena and Poseidon, coming down on the side of Athena. Athena possessed two contradictory qualities: as goddess of war, which she glorified, she became intoxicated by the cries of battle, while as goddess of wisdom and patron of the arts, she instructed people in the art of weaving and extracting oil from olives. On the occasion of the naming of the city, she donated an olive tree to the Athenians, which she is said to have planted in the internal courtyard of Erechtheion.

The exact year of the founding of Athens is uncertain. A clue can be found in the fortification of the Acropolis around 1400 BC. This rampart – some ruins of which remain today - protects the temples and altars built around the Acropolis hill, which date back to the initial settlement of Athens. According to legends, King Theseus united the Attican communities to create this first city-state. Theseus defeated the Minotaur, a monster with the head of a bull and the body of a man which belonged to King Minos of Crete. For nine consecutive years, the Athenians had had to bring seven young men and seven virgins to Minos every year in order to feed his creature, which he kept in the labyrinth of Knossos.

Herodotus tells of Doric migrations that occurred in three destructive waves (1250 and 1150 BC), when foreign tribes from the Balkans invaded the area around Athens. The city of Athens resisted the invaders and, unlike the cities of Mycene and Pylos, which were destroyed, managed to remain intact. As Athens was unable to accommodate all the refugees, many were forced to emigrate to a newly founded colony on the other side of the Aegean Sea, which became known as Ionia. The people now called Ionians are a diverse mixture of various tribes, who according to Herodotus, "...believed themselves to be the noblest of their species, they did not emigrate with their women, but married Carian women, whose parents they had previously killed".

10. Aphrodite, Pan and Eros, marble statues, Archaeological Museum, Athens.

The Trojan War

One of the most important literary events, not only for Greece but also for the cultural and scientific heritage of the rest of the world, was the appearance of the epic poems the *Iliad*, which tells of the events during the last year of the Trojan War (c. 1250 BC), and the *Odyssey*, which describes the detours and diversions of Odysseus on his journey home to Ithaca and to his wife Penelope. Both of these works were written by the poet Homer sometime between 750 and 700 BC. Between their transcription and the events they describe, there is a gap of 500 years during which travelling storytellers told the story of these heroic events, undoubtedly making numerous embellishments in the process.

The *Iliad* recounts the story of the Trojan War, which went on for many years - whether or not for 10 is still a matter of debate today – and during which the fortified city was besieged and finally completely destroyed by the Greeks. This was their revenge for the kidnapping of the beautiful Helen by Paris, son of Priam, King of Troy. The kidnapping was originally inspired by an argument between the three goddesses Hera, Athena and Aphrodite, as to who deserved the title of most beautiful goddess. To settle this quarrel, they asked for Paris' opinion, whereupon each goddess tried to seduce him with promises and expensive presents. He judged in favour of Aphrodite, who in return promised him the love of Helen, the most beautiful woman in the Greek world. Paris kidnapped her from the arms of her husband Menelaus, who immediately set about seeking revenge. The tragedy was thus inevitable. Many Greek heroes died in the war. The fortunes of battle kept passing from one side to the other and the gods passionately took part in the conflicts, protecting their favourites among the heroes. The war finally ended thanks to Odysseus, who feigned a retreat by the Greeks, leaving a large wooden horse as a sign of recognition for the long and brave defence of the city by its inhabitants. The Trojans, after intense discussion, eventually considered this to be a gift and dragged it inside the city walls, paying no heed to the repeated warnings of the prophetess Cassandra. Their downfall was thus assured since, hidden in the hollowed-out belly of the horse, the bravest of the Greek warriors were waiting. They remained there until darkness and then surprised the Trojans in their sleep, killing them and razing the city to the ground.

After the destruction of Troy, which had, at that time, a population of about 10,000, the Greeks returned home. However, Odysseus, because of his reckless behaviour and excessive fervour in battle, had angered the gods and was condemned by them to wander the seas for another ten years. He was to encounter many dangers before he was allowed to return home to Ithaca, to his wife Penelope. The *Odyssey* describes these adventures, ending with his arrival back in Ithaca. On his return, however, one more task awaited him as he had to vanquish his faithful wife Penelope's many admirers, who had treacherously tried to take his wife, his house, and his possessions during his 20-year absence. After this final trial of strength, Odysseus was at last allowed to grow old in peace in his homeland.

11. Jacques-Louis David, *The love of Paris and Helena*, 1799, Oil on canvas, 147 x 180 cm. Louvre, Paris.

Forms of government in Athens

Until the end of the 6th century, there were no towns as we understand them in Attica, but settlements in which the lords – the nobility – were representatives of their subjects before the gods and their chiefs in time of war. The monarchy, which still existed at the time of the great migrations, was peacefully removed from power and replaced by the Polis, the city-state which, within the confines of its clear boundaries, easily managed to organize itself.

After about the 8th century BC, the nobility that originated from Attica, the memory of the deeds of heroes such as Heracles fresh in its collective mind, took power in Athens and introduced a new form of government, the aristocracy. However, there were important changes made afterwards to the constitution due to reforms introduced first by Solon, a noble and learned trader who travelled widely throughout the then known world and who is said to have been elected as head of state, and then by Archon in 594 BC. These changes in the constitution opened the way for democracy in Athens. From this moment on, all free men, even those without means, could now take part in the meeting at which nine archons were elected for a period of office of one year. The highest-ranking archon was at the same time head judge; one was head of the armed forces; another was given responsibility for religious affairs and the other six looked after legal matters. The yearly report, which they had to give had to be approved at the general meeting. This then got them elected to the council of ex-archons, the Areiopagos, whose central task was to act as guardian of the laws. Only after the proclamation of a democratic constitution did Athens evolve into the cultural and political centre of the country.

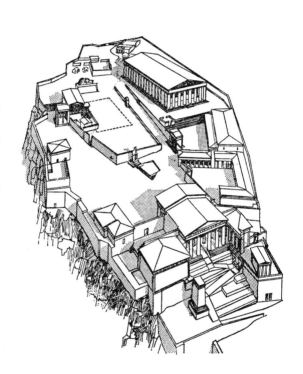

12. Horizontal projection of a temple / a drawing of the Acropolis as it was during the 5th century BC.

13. Head of Alexander the Great, Acropolis Museum, Athens.

Four centuries BC and after

The following centuries until the beginning of the modern era were times of contrast. On the one hand, Athens was flourishing in the spheres of art and culture. On the other, the city had to defend itself against two Persian military expeditions. (In 490 BC the Persians were defeated in Marathon, but in 480 BC the Persians conquered Athens and the Acropolis. Only in 479 BC were the Persians finally defeated in two great battles). Athens was at war with Sparta and lost military hegemony after its defeat in the Peloponnesian War (431- 404 BC). The city was occupied several times by various conquerors, destroyed and then rebuilt. Despite this turmoil, it was a golden age for the sciences, with a number of famous historical figures making their mark, including mathematicians such as Pythagoras, Euclid and the slightly younger Archimedes, the discoveries of whom still form the basis of mathematics today. The humanities were evolving and developing under the influence of great dramatists such as Aeschylus and Sophocles, and the philosophers Socrates and Plato.

14. View of the Acropolis and the Parthenon.

Famous generals such as Alexander the Great and Miltiades were the embodiment of the golden age of ancient Athens. The Periclean age, which lasted until the final third of the 5th century, brought fame to the city of Athens once again. Pericles oversaw the restoration of the Acropolis after the Persians, led by Xerxes, had sacked Athens and destroyed its temples. The city wall and residential quarters were also renovated (the city already had, at that time, at least 150,000 inhabitants). Supporting walls considerably extended the area covered by the Acropolis. The first temple to be built was the Parthenon (447 - 432 BC), and then the Propylaeum (437 - 432 BC). In 432, a temple in honour of the god Nike was added and in 421, the Erechtheion was built. Next to the Acropolis, at around the same time as the Parthenon, a temple in honour of Hephaistos and Athena was built. It was a time of many varied construction projects. In addition to the buildings already mentioned, work was also being carried out on the road to the important harbour of Piraeus situated nearby, and in the city of Piraeus itself. Pericles, as well as assuring the reconstruction of Athens, followed the tradition of Solon. He introduced democracy, a system of power based on the consent of the majority of the people.

All people were now equal before the law. Poverty was no longer an excuse for excluding anyone from public life, and the only criterion for judging a free, politically aware person was his personal ability. In the second half of the 4th century the Greeks, led by Alexander the Great, conquered the majority of the then known world and hellenized it. Two hundred years later, Greece fell into the hands of the Romans, under whose rule they remained until the disintegration of the Roman Empire.

After the change of era from BC to AD, the name of the apostle Paul, who lived and preached in Athens, starts to figure in Athenian history, as does that of the Roman emperor Hadrian in the 2nd century AD. In 330 AD, the Emperor Constantine moved the capital of the Roman Empire to Constantinople, a fertile soil for the Christian civilization, and thus founded the eastern Roman Empire, the cultural influences of which were basically Greek and which was later referred to as the Byzantine Empire. Byzantium fell into the hands of the Turks in 1453, and remained under Ottoman rule for almost four hundred years; the Greeks rebelled in 1821 and acquired independence in 1828 by force of arms.

15. The Parthenon.

This turbulent course of history is reflected in the transformation of the temples into churches, and then from churches into mosques, ending with the destruction of the Parthenon by Venetian grenades. Modern Greek history begins with the conquest of Athens in the 19th century by the rebel Greeks and the liberation of Nauplion in 1822.

16. Theatrical performance in the Odeon by Herodes Atticus.

Nauplion remained the capital of Greece until 1834, after which Athens was proclaimed capital of Greece by King Otto I. One of the most famous citizens of Athens at that time was Heinrich Schliemann, who was responsible for the first archeological excavations of Troy and other Greek cities. Not less important is the fact that the first Olympic games of the modern era were held in Athens in 1896. The winners are still commemorated today on a marble plaque in the old Olympic stadium. Athens' fate continued to fluctuate into the 20th century, with wars and revolts, victories and defeats, and with the political transition from monarchy to republic. The city of Athens enjoyed continuous prosperity even during its defeat at the hands of the Turks in 1922. Being a university town, and the seat of the government, the king and the parliament as well as that of the Orthodox and Roman Catholic archbishops,

Athens was always the political, religious and economic centre of Greece. Furthermore, the names of Melina Mercouri, Mikis Theodorakis and Andreas Papandreou became known around the world and even today remain symbolic of the Greek struggles against the dictatorship that held sway in the 1970s. Since the return to democracy in 1974, the abolition of the monarchy in 1975 and the acceptance of the constitution in the same year, Greece has been a parliamentary democracy with a presidential head of state.

17. View of the Acropolis and the Lykabettos hill.

Temples and Theatres

As in many countries, there are a lot of fortified locations in Greece today - fortresses, city walls and other public buildings and halls. But there are two particular types of building - the temple and the theatre – at which the Greeks have excelled, inspiring the rest of the world with its creations.

18. The Acropolis and the Parthenon.
19. *Metamorphosis tu Sotiros*, a small church with cruciform cupola at the foot of the Acropolis.
20. The Temple of Athena Nike.
21. A bench in front of the *Metamorphosis* church.

It is easy to imagine a scene from the most ancient past: a circular area made of flattened or paved earth with, in its centre, a vertical pole to which a beast is attached by a rope.

Constantly driven around the pole, the beast tramples the grain spread out on this threshing area, separating the wheat from the chaff. However, in this same spot, after the work was done, or on holidays, performances of country dancing were staged, and the place was thronged by singers and, later on, by orators. As the number of participants increased, so did the number of spectators, sitting perhaps on higher slopes arranged in a circle or a semicircle around the entertainers. At that time, there were no enclosed buildings in which to hold such spectacles: everything took place in the open air. But with the ever-increasing number of spectators, a type of semicircular stone bowl evolved from this early form of theatre and resulted in the arrangement of the spectators in rows and the addition of a high wall behind the stage. Not only is the architecture of these early theatres amazing but also their acoustics, which enabled a whispered script to be heard even in the highest seats. This is proof of the Greeks' incredible technical mastery. The function of the temples and their profound cultural significance

22. The Cariatids of the Erechtheion.

23. View of the rear façade of the Erechtheion.

was completely different to that of other secular buildings and can only be understood by looking at the relationship between the Greeks and the gods to whom the temples were dedicated.

In the beginning, these buildings consisted only of an altar where people worshipped the god who was personified by one of the elemental forces – sea, sun, thunder or lightning. It was only later that the early Greeks started to construct images of these gods. It then became necessary, in order to protect the image of the god placed within the altar, to construct a building around it. This arrangement is believed to have begun around the time of Homer. The dimensions of the oldest known Greek temples are about 100 ft long and 20 ft wide (approximately 35 by 6.5 metres). A wooden hall would consist of two naves divided by a central row of columns that bears the weight of a slightly sloping roof. There are no enclosed spaces in the early temples. It is a house without rooms, so to speak, bordered on all four sides by a triangular gable above enormous columns, first Doric, then Ionic. The temple was thus differentiated from all other buildings, which were usually constructed from bricks dried out in the open air. No other building had a roof placed above columns.

24. The Erechtheion.

It was not until several centuries later that royal palaces and houses of high-ranking citizens were embellished with columns at the front, and sometimes even at the back, to demonstrate the owner's power and wealth.

Two other characteristics distinguished the temples from secular buildings. The first of these was the high and uninterrupted flight of stairs, not designed for mere mortals to tread, whose top step spread to merge with the floor of the temple. The columns were placed on top of it, thus not requiring foundations of their own, and in between them stood statues consecrated to the particular god to whom the temple was dedicated. The other characteristic was the figurative decorations adorning the outside and the frieze surrounding the exterior gallery under the ceiling. Afterwards, rooms were added to this basic architecture and formed the external shell for the interior of the temple, the *naos* or *cella*. At the front or back of the temple there was a room of varying size, which held treasures dedicated to the god. It was only during the time of the construction of the Parthenon, around the middle of the 5th century, that the builders found another way of harmonizing the size of the side walls with that of the facing walls. The relation between the width and the length, in the case of the Hephaistos temple, for example, is 6 columns wide to 13 columns long, compared to that of the Parthenon, which is 8 columns wide to 17 columns in length.

The *naos* or *cella* of the Hephaistos temple, which was heightened by an additional step with 6 columns in length and 4 columns in width, also had a front and back chamber of two columns each. In comparison, the Parthenon's *naos* was heightened by two steps with 9 columns in length and 5 columns in width to become a small salon with a rear chamber supported on four columns.

25. Ionian capital of the Erechtheion.
26. The pediment of the temple.

27. The Parthenon.

28. A = Doric,
B = Volute, C = Ionic,
and D = Corinthian capital.

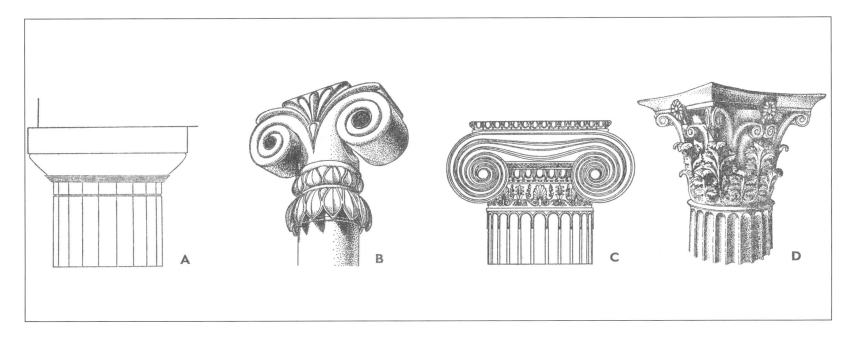

29. The Parthenon.

It has long been a subject of academic debate as to which of these two great temples, the Parthenon or the Hephaistos, is the oldest. However, because of the Parthenon's greater width of 2 columns and thus its more imposing and more monumental nature, it definitely has the edge over the Hephaistos temple. It is estimated that the master builders Iktionos and Kallikrates designed the Parthenon between 447 and 432. It was the job of Phidias, who was one of the great classical Greek artists, to supply the icon of the god which was, as in other temples, located in the *naos*.

The Greeks did not invent this type of architecture but borrowed it from the Egyptians. However, the Greeks developed the shape of the shafts of the columns and of their bases and capitals, of which the simplest was the Doric capital with its sleek rising curves. The volute capital, with buttresses on both sides and decorated with pendant leaves, is the predecessor of the Ionic capital in which the volutes are continuously linked together in the middle of the column. On the Corinthian capital, the volutes are combined with acanthus leaves and form an extensive decoration of the column.

The temples constructed on the Acropolis were each dedicated to one specific god. However, the Erechtheion, designed in Ionic style and situated to the north of the Parthenon, was host to about five different cults. None of the temples permitted other buildings to be constructed nearby. All of them stood alone, wide, imposing and balanced in shape. People approaching the temple and the god therein fell silent out of respect. We can only imagine how the Greeks felt at the sight of their temple and what their gods meant to them.

Goethe understood and shared this respect for temples and wrote to Herder: "It is the most supreme and glorious idea and I would like to take it back north with me just the way it is".

The Christians, however, showed little respect for these buildings, particularly the Parthenon, and renamed it, using it for more than 500 years as St. Mary's church and destroying the eastern gable and possibly also some metopes. In the 15th century, the Turks first transformed it into a mosque with a minaret and later placed a gunpowder store in it, which was blown up in 1687 by a Venetian grenade, destroying several parts of the temple in the process.

Tour of the city

The Acropolis

30. The Parthenon by night.
31. The Parthenon.

No visit to Athens would be complete without a visit to the famous Acropolis, which was already inhabited and fortified in the second millennium BC. The religious centre of early Athens is situated on the flattened summit of the rock with steep slopes on three sides. If you select the path up from the old town you will pass right in front of a small cruciform cupola, the *Metamorphosis tu Sotiros*, a church built in the 14th century, and you can rest from the uphill climb on a bench. Continuing upwards, after the ticket office at the entrance, one reaches the imposing marble steps of the Propylae built from 437 to 432 BC, which served as the entrance to this holy place. With their unusual combination of enormous Doric and Ionic columns, constructed of marble from a quarry near Athens, they dominate the entrance and are astonishing for their incredible dimensions. In their centre stands a wall with five passages between the columns and an entrance hall situated on the west side along with other side buildings, which once contained a collection of icons that are now preserved in the Pinakotheque.

The Propylae served as the major portal to the sanctuary, but also functioned as a meeting place and occasionally as a gallery for artists; afterwards, they were additionally used for defensive purposes, being quite often chosen as the command post.

From this vantage point there is a wonderful panorama of Athens. In front of the Propylae, on a small rock, stands an elegant temple, which was constructed between 432 and 421 BC during the war against Sparta and consecrated to the wingless goddess of victory Nike. With its four columns at the front and back, it is one of the most accomplished examples of the Ionian style and, like the Erechtheion, manages to use the necessity of adapting to cope with its difficult setting to create impressive architecture.

The asymmetrical Erechtheion, which differs from the usual rectangular shape and was erected between 421 and 406 BC in the same delicate Ionian style, is seen as an enigma of classical Greek architecture due to three unusual elements in its construction: two different foundation levels, four arrangements of columns and the ceiling of the south hall supported by six female statues (Caryatids). This temple was the centre of Athenian worship and was designed by its builders to remind people of the legendary king Erechtheus, whose palace had once stood near this place. Under one corner of the Erechtheion lies the tomb of the first Athenian king, Cecrops. In one of the courts stood an olive tree that Athena was reputed to have given to the city during the dispute over its name. On the northern side, it supposedly used to be possible to see through an opening in the earth the traces of the red-hot trident with which Poseidon is said to have split the rock, causing a saltwater spring to flow from it. The Erechtheion housed the icon of the goddess Athena and altars for Poseidon and Hephaistos. In the Caryatid hall, the ritual of changing clothing took place after the end of the pan-Athenian procession. The Caryatids which can be seen today are mere reproductions; the originals are in the Acropolis museum behind glass, while there is another in the British Museum in London.

Of the six Ionian columns in the eastern hall – the northern hall likewise had six columns – only five remain. The sixth column is to be found in London, where Lord Elgin placed it along with other "souvenirs" – the Elgin Marbles.

The Erechtheion appears to have fascinated its various owners: the western hall had a change of use in the 7th century to a two-storey Christian church, and in the 15th century the Turkish commander of the fortress – perhaps inspired by the Caryatids – installed his harem.

If one arrives at the Erechtheion by crossing the Sacred Way, which traverses the Acropolis Museum and the Propylae from east to west, one reaches the temple of Athena Parthenos, the Parthenon. At first glance, one is impressed primarily by the grandness of the building, but after looking more closely one can see the traces of its gradual destruction, caused not only by environmental pollution and the infamous Athenian smog, but also by the constantly increasing number of visitors. For this reason the Acropolis is again under construction, and will always remain so. With the help of internal scaffolding and equipment designed to handle the large blocks of stone and column sections, the Parthenon is gradually being restored. Looking at the construction workers at their work, one wonders how this building could have been created 2,400 years ago with such precision without the benefit of our modern technical instruments. For many, this sight only serves to increase the respect which they feel for the ancient builders of this monument. However, the restorers have not completely followed the original model: many temples which were colourfully painted are left today as plain marble.

32. Statue of Athena in the temple of Athena.
33. Sphinx (550 BC).
34. The bearer of the calf, Acropolis Museum, Athens.

Apparently rectangular on the exterior, this Doric temple, dedicated to the virgin goddess Athena and constructed entirely of marble, is distinguished by a number of features: the horizontal lines curve from the corners to the centre, the slim columns are swollen in the middle, while the top decreases and tilts delicately inwards. All of this put together, with the grooves in the columns that narrow in at the top, gives the form of the building an unexpected lightness.

In the two-storey *naos* or *cella* there once stood a statue of the goddess armed with a lance and shield which was created by the sculptor Phidias who worked under the supervision of Pericles. This formed the religious centre of the Parthenon. The statue was made of wood, while its clothing was made of about 1,000 kg of gold, and the face and hands of ivory. It was later taken to Constantinople, where it disappeared sometime between the 6th and 10th centuries. We only know that this statue even existed thanks to smaller copies that have been preserved. Reproductions show the goddess with a statue of Nike in her right hand, a sphinx on her helmet and an ivory Medusa on her breast.

Those who envied Phidias grouped themselves against him by claiming that he had become rich by keeping some of the gold from the luxurious decoration for himself. Since the gold leaf covering was restricted to specific areas of the statue, it was easy to check the weight of the gold and thus prove his innocence. However, he was forced to leave Athens anyway. On the exterior wall of the *naos* there is a sculpted frieze. Judging from its 160-metre length, one can easily imagine the size of the *naos* itself. Behind it there is a two-storey chamber in which the treasures of the temple were kept.

Here stood the throne of Xerxes, with its silver feet, from which he observed the defeat of his navy at Salamis (480 BC).

35. Reconstruction of the western gable end of the Parthenon; Nike and Amphitrite rein in the horses to prevent them from rearing.

The grandiose decoration of the temple is not limited to the *naos*, but continues with the surrounding frieze and the gable ends at the front and back of the Parthenon. The sculptures, which were created by a number of artists under the supervision of Phidias, are striking in their presentation and disposition. The metope plaques show events from Greek history and mythology: on the eastern side the gods are defeating the giants, on the western side the Greeks defeat the Amazons, on the south side, which is the best preserved, the battle against the centaurs is depicted, and the north side shows the Trojan War.

Many amazing artistic items from the 6th and 5th centuries BC are kept in the rooms of the Acropolis Museum. Apart from the friezes and marble facings, the most famous statues or sculptures must include, amongst others, the head of Alexander the Great, the Sphinx, the young Kritios and the Calf Bearer. One should also mention the relief of the Youths in Cloaks, the Group of Unclothed Youths, and the Lioness Feeding the Calf, all incredible works of art.

36. Herodes Atticus' Odeon.

Two Theatres

Before arriving at the Acropolis itself, one can see the restored amphitheatre below the Odeon (a music hall) of Herodes Atticus, constructed in Roman style in 161 AD, 600 years after the Pericles building of the Acropolis. Here there were musical competitions,

37. Herodes Atticus' Odeon by moonlight.

and the white marble steps could seat about 5,000 spectators during the Athenian summer festivals. The stage wall was once as high as the surrounding wall of the amphitheatre. Its many window-shaped openings look out over the town and the hill standing opposite with its monument to Philopappos. From this monument, erected between 114 and 116 BC in honour of the Roman philanthropist Gaius Julius Antiochos Philopappos, the visitor has a beautiful panoramic view of the plain of Attica.

Furthermore, from the southern slope of the Acropolis one can easily see down to another theatre, the theatre of Dionysos, which was completed in the 4th century BC (earlier forms date from the 6th and 5th centuries), which is part of the Dionysos-Eleuthereus sanctuary. However, its current form originated essentially during Roman times. Ancient comedies and tragedies by the great Greek poets were presented here. Today, the names of Aeschylus, Sophocles and Euripides are still universally known and their tragedies still belong to the repertoires of modern theatre. However, the origins of Greek drama remain unknown. They perhaps evolved from earlier forms of dances and songs in honour of Dionysus, the god of wine. These dances and songs were included in the heroic epics of the time, which then developed into ritual tragedies performed for the whole population during Dionysian feast days and financed by the rich citizens of Athens. The sculptures in the theatre depicted, among other things, the god Dionysus himself. The priest participated in the performance sitting on a marble seat of honour. About 17,000 spectators could be accommodated in the theatre, with seats that reached as high as the rock of the Acropolis, many traces of which can still be seen.

38. Herodes Atticus' Odeon.
39. The Amphitheatre of Dionysus.

40. The Greeka Agora : Thisseum.

41. Frieze at the rear of the temple of Hephaistos.

42. The Temple of Hephaistos.

43. The Greek Agora :
sarcophagus.

The Areiopagos

44. The Greek Agora : Tholos (Rotunda).

Slightly to the west of the Acropolis is the Areiopagos, the hill of Ares, where the council of the Ex-Archons, the council of the Best, used to meet. It was a higher court, where those accused of murder were tried and which also dealt with rebels. Saint Paul is said to have preached the gospel here to his Athenian audience. Today all one can see is a partly uncovered excavation site with a street and the remains of some houses.

45. The Greek Agora :
 head of Nike.
46. The Greek Agora :
 middle hall.

47. The Greek Agora :
Attalos Stoa.

48. The Attalos Stoa :
Ionian row
of columns.

49. The Attalos Stoa :
the Kneeler.

The Greek Agora

To the north of the Areiopagos stretches the area of the Agora. This is where the ancient market place and the centre of Athens were once located. The area has been settled since prehistoric times and has always been one of the two public and economic centres of the city, the other being the Acropolis. Schools, tribunals and government buildings were to be found here. During excavations of the southern part, several workshops belonging for example to cobblers and masons, were found. Two buildings now dominate the area: the Attalos Stoa to the east of the area beside the Pan-Athenian Way (upon which every four years there was a festival procession in honour of the goddess Athena's birthday) and the Hephaistos temple located further to the west (previously erroneously called the Theseion).

The reconstructed Attalos Stoa, named after king Attalos of Pergamon (159 - 138 BC) who founded it, is an impressive two-storey, 116-metre long hall, surrounded by an external Doric and an internal Ionian row of columns. These rows of columns served either as an area for shaded promenades or for drifting around the shops located here. Since its construction, the Stoa has been used as a museum for the exhibition of the sculptures which had been found during the excavations of the Agora area (in the vestibule), and of objects of everyday life associated with the activities taking place in the Agora. Among the sculptures in the vestibule, the head of Triton, created around 150 BC, a torso, and the large statue of Apollon Patroos (4th century BC), particularly stand out.

50. The Attalos Stoa : the Agei Apostoli.

51. Fresco in the Agei Apostoli.

In the rooms of the museum one can admire the head of Nike, the figure of a young satyr, the figure of The Kneeler and a basin in a glass case in which Leda and the Swan can be observed. In the south of the Attalos Stoa the remains of the Valerian Wall, dating from the 3rd century AD, can still be seen.

The Hephaistos temple, situated on the hill of Kolonos Agoraios, was built during the 5th century BC and was dedicated to the god of fire and craftsmen, who was repudiated by his mother Hera. This temple is the best preserved example of the Doric style. Although built at approximately the same time as the Parthenon, it cannot compare with the Parthenon's size, elegance or artistic expression, due to the proportion of its columns (6 to 13). Since it is undergoing restoration, one can only admire the outside, particularly the fragments of relief on the metopes, on the east and west sides. A little further away, beyond the western side of the temple, some sarcophagi are still on display, and the reliefs which decorate them are in better condition. Below the Hephaistos temple is the Tholos, constructed in approximately 465 BC, which once contained a sacred fire at its centre, today marked by a stone, and which served as a round meeting room.

52. The Roman Agora and the Tower of the Winds.

Continuing along the way, one reaches the remains of the middle hall, in front of which was the Odeon or music hall of Agrippa, and beside this the beautifully preserved capital of the Odeon of Agrippa. At the southeastern exit, a little hidden away, stands the Agii Apostoli from the 11th century, with its beautiful external mural and several well-preserved frescoes inside.

The Roman Agora

To the east of the Greek Agora, separated from it by what was once a street and directly beside the Tower of the Winds, is what used to be the Roman Agora. Building was begun by Julius Caesar (100 to 44 BC) and finished by the emperors Trajan and Hadrian. It is a square of about 11,000 m^2, which served as a market place with a Stoa, of which only the remains of the Ionian columns can be seen today. One can still easily recognize the remains of the communal latrine with its row of marble seats. Immediately to its rear were the public baths. In the excavation site are some beautifully ornamented sarcophagi.

The Tower of the Winds

53. Old marketplace in the Roman Agora.

54. Detail of the Tower of the Winds.

55. The Roman Agora and the Tower of the Winds.

Part of the area around the Roman Agora contains the octagonal Tower of the Winds, which stands approximately 12 metres high and was erected in the middle of the 1st century BC. The first Athens museum operated here. Originally, it had a sundial on each of its eight faces underneath a frieze. The relief shows the eight gods of the winds. In the turret there is an alcove for a highly elaborate water clock with a complicated tube system.

The Hadrian Library

To the north of the Roman Agora and right beside the mosque is the site of the Hadrian Library, named after its founder and built around 132 AD, with a Christian basilica built on top of it in the 6th century. Hadrian was not only an emperor, but also a poet and an author. Unfortunately, his works did not survive. The most significant finding that one can observe on the excavation site is the Propylon, consisting of 4 columns and an interesting exterior wall with some astonishingly well-preserved frescoes on the inside.

56. The Tower of the Winds.

57. The Roman Agora : sarcophagus.

Next pages :

58. Hadrian's Library.

59. The Olympeion, the temple of Zeus the Olympian.

60. Row of columns in the Olympeion.

61. The Olympeion.

The Olympeion

Looking down from the Acropolis, one immediately sees the Olympeion, the temple of Zeus of Olympus and the largest temple in Corinthian style in Greece. Its construction took around 700 years, with several interruptions, until it was completed under the emperor Hadrian in 131 AD. At the entrance to the site there are a few remains of columns and, further away, lie the remains of some houses and of a Roman bathhouse. The thirteen remaining enormous vertical columns, which can be seen from a distance, are still in good condition. Somewhat further away stand two individual columns, and one lies broken in front of them in a way that gives an approximate idea of the dimensions of the temple. At the edge of the excavation site is the well-preserved Hadrian gate that marks the boundary between Theseus, the old city, and the new city of Hadrian.

62. Antique Olympic Stadium.

63. Antique Olympic Stadium.

64. Plaque commemorating Olympic cities since 1896.

The Olympic stadium

The Olympic stadium was first constructed in 330 BC for the Pan-Athenian games and was used afterwards by the Romans for their spectacles. Herodes Atticus sumptuously renovated it, however its condition declined after the Byzantine period and was only renovated to its present form in 1895 for the Olympic games which were held in the following year. A marble plaque at the entrance commemorates these first games of the modern era. The stadium was built according to ancient models as a rectangular surface of about 190 metres in length and 30 metres in width. This shape was originally designed to accommodate the types of sports engaged in by the naked competitors: there were races of one length of the stadium, and of two or twenty lengths. The two-length race was unique since the competitors had to carry a helmet and a shield as they ran. In ancient times, the first Olympic games were held in 776 BC and were most certainly religious in origin. One could consider the games that Achilles organized in memory of his friend Patrocles, who was killed by Hector during the battle of Troy, as the forerunner of all Olympic games. (Achilles later killed Hector and was then killed by Paris whose arrow wounded his heel, which was the only vulnerable part of his body). In 394 AD Theodosius I forbade the games. Today the stadium can seat, on its white marble benches, about 60,000 spectators. A marble plaque at the entrance commemorates host cities for the Olympic games up until 1988.

776 πΧ — 1894 μΧ

ΟΛΥΜΠΙΑΔΕΣ

Α	ΑΘΗΝΑΙ	1896
Β	ΠΑΡΙΣΙΟΙ	1900
Γ	ΑΓ. ΛΟΥΔΟΒΙΚΟΣ	1904
Δ	ΛΟΝΔΙΝΟΝ	1908
Ε	ΣΤΟΚΧΟΛΜΗ	1912
ΣΤ	ΔΕΝ ΕΤΕΛΕΣΘΗ	1916
Ζ	ΑΜΒΕΡΣΑ	1920
Η	ΠΑΡΙΣΙΟΙ	1924
Θ	ΑΜΣΤΕΡΔΑΜ	1928
Ι	ΛΟΣ ΑΝΤΖΕΛΕΣ	1932
ΙΑ	ΒΕΡΟΛΙΝΟΝ	1936
ΙΒ	ΔΕΝ ΕΤΕΛΕΣΘΗ	1940
ΙΓ	ΔΕΝ ΕΤΕΛΕΣΘΗ	1944
ΙΔ	ΛΟΝΔΙΝΟΝ	1948
ΙΕ	ΕΛΣΙΝΚΙ	1952
ΙΣΤ	ΜΕΛΒΟΥΡΝΗ	1956
ΙΖ	ΡΩΜΗ	1960
ΙΗ	ΤΟΚΥΟ	1964
ΙΘ	ΜΕΞΙΚΟΝ	1968
Κ	ΜΟΝΑΧΟΝ	1972
ΚΑ	ΜΟΝΤΡΕΑΛ	1976
ΚΒ	ΜΟΣΧΑ	1980
ΚΓ	ΛΟΣ ΑΝΤΖΕΛΕΣ	1984
ΚΔ	ΣΕΟΥΛ	1988

The Plaka

To the north, beneath the Acropolis, is the quarter known as the Plaka, now a conservation area where one can find remnants of ancient times. It was founded by the Turks and is regarded as the oldest part of Athens. In the picturesque lanes, with their simple houses in shaded squares, as well as the taverns and souvenir shops which are open until almost midnight, one can find everything from plaster figurines and T-shirts to icons. Here, the lottery ticket and chestnut sellers, shoe cleaners and pavement artists await their customers, and anyone who might want to have a tattoo painted on their body will find a tattoo artist to do the job. The shopkeepers and vendors are friendly and it is easy to strike up a friendly conversation. If you are lucky enough, you will find a tavern with a roaring fire, where sausages flambéed in ouzo are served or where a band plays to accompany your meal. During the day tourists rule, but in the evening the Athenians gladly come here to listen to the singers in the tiny restaurants. And if enough of the Retsina, which is served from a barrel until late in the evening, has been drunk, then one might catch a few tourists bravely risking a few steps of the Sirtaki dance.

65. Plaka, the oldest quarter of Athens and is a protected patrimony.

66. A bicycle near a door in Plaka.

67. Two men conversing in
    Plaka.
68. Souvenir shops in Plaka.
69. A shoe cleaner in Plaka.

70. Basketware on sale in Plaka.

71. A sweets seller in Plaka.

72. A traditional dance performance.

Next page :

73. Shutters with vines in Plaka.

At the edge of the Plaka, right under the Acropolis, is the small excavation site of the only remaining Choragus monument in Athens. The Choragusi were the sponsors who paid for the chorus who performed in tragedies and, in return, a monument was dedicated to them.

74. Streets in Plaka.

75. A beautiful street with houses in Plaka.

In this case, the monument, situated at the end of a lane in a small excavation site, is dedicated to Lysikrates. The spaces between the Corinthian columns are filled with round marble plaques. However, there are only traces of the capitals remaining.

76. The Daphni restaurant. The walls and the stairway of the Daphni, a restaurant famous for its walls covered in Byzantine frescos. It is located in the Plaka Quarter of Athens.

77. Streets in Plaka.

The Cathedral and churches

Alongside Athens' modern cathedral, the Great Metropolitan, there are also a number of other smaller churches worth visiting. The Great Metropolitan is being restored at the moment and inside there is steel scaffolding which unfortunately obscures part of the décor, but is otherwise well worth seeing. Above the entrance, guarded by two marble lions, is a beautiful mosaic of the Annunciation, and inside there are some magnificent embossed silver decorations.

Right beside the Grand Metropolitan is the Lesser Metropolitan (closed most of the time), which is one of the most beautiful Byzantine monuments in the city. It was constructed from material left over from ancient and medieval buildings, so-called 'spoils'. On the external walls, magnificent reliefs sit alongside a calendar frieze and several carved figures.

In the centre of the town are some other churches which are worth a visit: in the middle of the pedestrian area is the Kapnikaréa church, with its cruciform cupola and a pretty mosaic above the entrance, while the Plaka quarter of town shelters the Orthodox-Byzantine church of St. Catherine, with its beautiful colours, and, in the centre of town, the Agii Theódori, with another cruciform cupola. All three churches date back to the 11ᵗʰ century. In the street leading to the cathedral is the tiny Agia Dynamis with a bell tower built beside it. It dates back to the 17ᵗʰ century and has a monastery building overlooking it.

78. The Great Metropolitan, Cathedral.

79. A traditional orthodox church service.

80. The Agia Dynamis.

The Kerameikos cemetery

To the west of the Greek Agora, formerly half inside and half outside of the city wall, but today in the vicinity of the Thissio metro station, is the Kerameikos cemetery, which is well worth a visit. Here you can find not only remains of the ancient city wall, built hastily by Themistocles in 478 BC, but also the two famous gates, the Dipylon and the Holy Gate, named after Holy Street, which stand right beside it. In ancient times, the famous Pan-Athenian Way led from the Dipylon into the city and along this route the heroes who had fallen in battle were carried to the cemetery, where they were buried. The graves mostly date back to the 5th and 4th centuries BC and have many beautiful gravestones (on the left once can see a female servant depicted presenting a jewellery box to the deceased, who is sitting on an elegantly decorated chair).

After visiting the cemetery one should also stop by the museum attached to it, where one can admire a variety of sculptures and excavation findings, including a relief of a group of horsemen at the base of a stele dating from around 640 BC, a sphinx from around 550 BC, and a marble bull straining to get free in the inner courtyard.

81. The main entrance to the famous old Kerameikos cemetery of Athens.

82. The Kerameikos cemetery.

83. Relief from a tomb in the Kerameikos cemetery.

84. The gravestone of Ampharete, Kerameikos Museum, Athens.

85. A tombstone in the Kerameikos cemetery.

86. The gravestone of Delixeos,
Kerameikos Museum,
Athens.

87. A tombstone in the
Kerameikos cemetery.

The Lykabettos

On a clear morning, the extraordinary view from the Lykabettos hill, which rises unmistakably from the bright labyrinth of houses at the centre of the city on the Acropolis by the Gulf of Saronikos, is a reward for those who have managed to conquer the almost 280-metre ascent on foot from the city below. The ascent is not so demanding if one takes advantage of the cable car for the first half of the journey. At the top of the hill is the small and much visited Agii Georgios chapel, built in 1834. Those taking the long route back can go through the Kolonaki quarter, situated at the foot of the hill and which shelters many small modern shops.

88. The Lykabettos, the Agii Georgios church.
89. The Syntagma square.
90. Athens' city centre.

The centre

After seeing so much that dates back to classical and ancient times, it is essential to catch a glimpse of modern Athens. One of the main centres of activity is the busy Syntagma Square, on whose benches, in the afternoons, people sit to enjoy the sun and watch others hurrying busily by. Here, at the western side of the square, is the modern metro station on the steps of which young people gather to meet. In display cases in the metro station findings from the various different excavations are shown.

Behind Syntagma Square, towards the east and beside a busy street, is the parliament building. It was originally conceived in the 1830s as a castle for King Otto I, but was transformed about 100 years later to serve its present function. With its neat classical façade and the ten Doric columns in the portico, it radiates power and dignity. In front of the building, set into the supporting wall of the area in front of the parliament, is the tomb of the Unknown Soldier. This is where the Euzone guards of honour parade. Directly beside the parliament is the vast, much visited National Garden, one of the essential green lungs of Athens, and which contains a large and prestigious building with a classical façade, the Zappeion, which is used for exhibitions.

Only a few minutes on foot north of the parliament is the Schliemann Museum, set up in the 1870s and called 'Iliou méla-thron' (the palace of Ilion ; 'Ilion' is the old name for Troy). With its two-storey lodge supported on columns, it is considered to be one of the most beautiful buildings in Athens. The archeologist Heinrich Schliemann believed he had discovered the location of ancient Troy and Mycenae and led the excavations, using Homer's writing to guide him.

Continuing in the same direction, we come to the so-called Neoclassical Trilogy, formed by the university and the neighbouring buildings of the Academy and National Library. The entrance to the university, with its two Ionian columns, is flanked by two sculptures. Above the door is a painting of Otto I, and on the square in front of it stands a fountain whose cool flow of water makes the summer heat more bearable. While the university was built from 1839 to1864, the construction of the Academy started in 1859 but took more than 25 years to be completed. This building is an exact marble copy of the parliament building in Vienna, and in its entrance area one can admire a particularly beautiful sculpture of Apollo and Athena. Equally of interest here are the coffer which stands in the vestibule, the frieze, and the lanterns on their pedestals. The third of these buildings is the National Library, built from 1887 to 1902, with its entrance hall supported by six Doric columns and a staircase elegantly ascending on both sides.

91. On the Syntagma square.

92. The Parliament building.
93. The changing of the guards
in front of the Presidium.

94. The Euzones' parade.
95. The Zappeion.

From here, the charming market to the west of the university is only a small walking distance away. The market offers the visitor an abundance of regional sea products, some of it still alive and often loudly advertised. In another uncovered part of the market one can buy flowers, spices, bags of fruit and vegetables, and a wide variety of other kinds of food. In the shops nearby one can find olives in all shapes and sizes, ranging from the brightest green to the darkest purple. Hams and sausages are hung up in rows or stacked in blocks. On the steps in front of the shops peasant women sit, offering for sale bulbs of garlic or simple objects like lighters or shoe-laces with which they try to earn a little extra to survive.

Not far from the market is the town hall with its four-columned portico and a vast forecourt broken up by a fountain and a modern sculpture as well as a small fenced–off excavation area at its eastern edge.

Coming back to the city, we arrive in Monastiráki Square, where the two main parallel shopping streets converge. One of them, the Mitropoleos, stretches from beyond the Cathedral to Syntagma Square, where the Athens Hotel, rich in Greek tradition, is situated. The square can also be reached by going down Ermou Street, with its beautiful shops and lack of traffic. In Ermou street, in the afternoon, performers entertain passers-by with a barrel organ or guitar music, or even mime, while hawkers with their handbags, lighters, sunglasses, textiles and other goods spread out their wares on the pavement and encourage you to stay. Amazingly, in many kiosks in this area one can purchase a huge variety of newspapers from different corners of the world, as well as drinks and ice cream. On the western edge of the Syntagma Square are several smaller cafés that have turned the pavement into a terrace with their tables and chairs, an inviting prospect after a busy day's shopping.

You can see everywhere the efforts that have been made to improve the appearance of the city, and not just to preserve the classical buildings. However, one can also see in the nearby streets the ugly carbuncles of abandoned facades.

96. The Schliemann Museum, called Iliou mélathron.
97. The Academy of Athens.

98. The Academy.
99. The National Library.

100. Resting on a park bench.

101. The town centre, with a cigarette lighter seller.

102. At the market, a confectionery seller.

Next pages :

103. An Old Greek woman in traditional Greek clothes enjoying an ice cream.

104. A Fish market.

105. At the market.

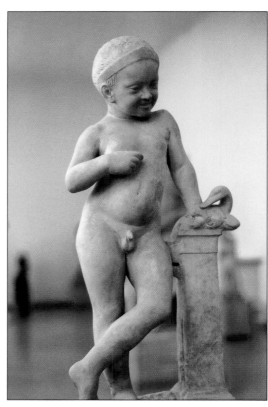

The Museums

North of the market halls is one of the most important museums, the National Archaeological Museum, which opened in 1860 and houses many priceless works of art which provide an incomparable overview of Greek art. The exhibitions start with the Neolithic period and end with late antiquity. The collection is so extensive that a single visit can only give a passing impression. It contains, to name only the most important, works from Archaic, Mycenaean and Cicladean art, classical sculpture, tomb monuments, vase collections, as well as black and red pottery. One of the many splendid pieces is a larger than life-sized bronze figure, found in the sea, of Zeus throwing a lightning bolt.

On one of the main roads leading out of the city is the Benaki Museum, with its collection of Greek golden jewellery, icons, craftwork and folk objects from around 1450 to 1900. But one can also admire two amazing 5,000-year-old gold vases, two paintings by the Spanish artist El Greco and many works by other painters.

The Byzantine Museum is only a few minutes away on foot from the Benaki Museum, and contains one of the most beautiful collections of icons, as well as sculptures and mosaics, from the 14th to the 18th century.

Continuing on, we come to the Museum of Cicladean Art with its marble works of art that are 4,000 to 5,000-years-old but yet seem so modern. Some are only 10 cm in size, others up to 150 cm.

On the way back to the centre of town, we pass the Military Museum, built by the Colonels who ruled the country between 1967 and 1974 and in front of which some ageing jet fighters are exhibited. Inside there are mostly pictures of the partisan battles during the Second World War.

In the Plaka area, there is a small and modern museum that focuses on Greek folk art with a remarkable, but yet slightly surprising, collection of carnival costumes from the island of Skiros.

Standing outside the National Gallery, with its works of Greek painting and sculpture, is a large sculpture made of glass, placed on a small lawn.

The National History Museum, which boasts an entrance hall supported by four columns (the front and rear entrances are the same in style) and a monument at the front dedicated to Kolokotrónis, a man who fought in the name of freedom, shows more recent Greek history. The Schliemann Museum is located nearby.

106. Mosaic, National Archaeological Museum, Athens.
107. Figure of boy, National Archaeological Museum, Athens.
108. The National Archaeological Museum, Athens.

109. The Fishing harbour of Mikrolimanos.

110. A ship near the shores of Pirée.

Piraeus

The former independent town of Piraeus is now a busy suburb of Athens with elegant shops. It can easily be reached from the centre by the Athenian metro, the Elektrikós, which in this case travels above ground. Along the way, one can get an impression of the suburbs of Athens. In the small, pretty fishing harbour of Mikrolimanos there are numerous fish restaurants situated around an almost perfectly circular quay, encouraging visitors to stay for an evening meal. They sell products freshly caught from the sea as well as from the many fish farms on the coast at a remarkable price. Sailing boats and beautiful yachts are moored at similarly circular sea marinas. Further west, near the railway station, is the large central harbour where the ferries, cruise liners and large cargo ships continually arrive and depart, to and from the islands.

111. The Fishing harbour of Mikrolimanos.

112. The Beach in the suburb
of Athens.

Epilogue

The restoration work which is currently being carried out on the cultural monuments of Athens requires a large financial investment. However, there remains a lot to be done in order to be prepared for the Olympic games in 2004. Athens, already a cultural capital of Europe two and a half thousand years ago, has preserved its culture with its world-famous monuments. In spite of all the historical changes the city has undergone, the Athenians are able to display their rich heritage to the people of the world, who greet it with wonder and amazement. Everyone who visits this city must feel the enormous debt owed to Athens for having left the marks of its culture on an entire continent.

113. A Church in Piraeus.

Greek Gods

The Greek pantheon is divided by historians into a number of groups. Those mentioned first are the pre-Olympian gods principally concerned with the creation of Greece – Gaia, Uranus, Chronos, Oceanus, Rhea, and Themis. During Zeus' reign over gods and mortals, the stories of the 12 Olympian gods, which have come to us in various forms, begin. These gods are the result of various unions between the pre-Olympian gods that preceded them:

Aphrodite, the goddess of love, beauty and fertility, was born from out of the surf. Paris chose her as the most beautiful of the goddesses and received, as a reward, the love of the beautiful Helen, whom he stole from her husband Menelaus; this led to the outbreak of the Trojan War. Aphrodite was married to Hephaistos, but had a colourful series of affairs not only with other gods, but also with some mortals. Hence, she was the lover of Zeus, of Ares and Adonis and mother of Eros, Anteros, Priapus, Aeneas, Hermaphroditus and Harmonia.

Apollo, the most handsome of the gods, son of Zeus and Leto and brother of Artemis, is not only the god of the day and of light, but also of music and poetry. He drives the chariot of the sun and is omniscient because he can see everything that happens on earth from his seat in the heavens. When Odysseus and his companions slaughtered the sacred cattle on the island of Sicily on their return voyage from Troy, Apollo complained to Zeus, who destroyed Odysseus' ship, leaving all of his companions to drown.

Ares is the god of war, son of Zeus and Hera. He is described as a violent and bloodthirsty god and as such enjoyed only a limited popularity. When Diomedes wounded him near Troy, he complained to his father Zeus, who fobbed him off by saying : "Don't bother me with your complaints, fickle one, you are the most hated of all the gods who live on Mount Olympus. Your only inclination is for war and conflict; you have the temperament of your mother, and if you were the son of some other god and not me, you would long ago have met the fate of Uranus' sons".

Artemis, the goddess of hunting, was the twin sister of Apollo. Because of her beauty she indulged in rivalry with Aphrodite. She is often characterized by her bow and arrow. She was the protector of virgins, and she in turn requested that her father Zeus grant her and her sister Hestia to remain virgins. She hunted with her companions, the Nymphs.

Athena is the permanently virginal goddess born from Zeus' head, who made her mark in ancient mythology because of her glorification of war. When she was born, the earth shook, Mount Olympus trembled and the sea raged, and because her first steps unleashed such powers, she remained fascinated by war and the hue and cry of battle. She was at the same time patron of the arts, goddess of wisdom and of crafts.

Eros is the god of love and is often represented in art as a boy with a bow.

Hades is the god of the underworld.

Hera, daughter of Chronos and Rhea, and wife of Zeus, is paradoxically the patron of marriage, even though she had to put up with her husbands endless philandering. She competed with Aphrodite and Athena for the title of most beautiful goddess. When Paris did not vote in her favour, she became a temperamental defender of the Greeks during the Trojan War.

Hermes, mischievous messenger of the gods, was originally a god of nature and shepherds. He was the son of Zeus and Maia, and the lover of Aphrodite. He was not only the god of traders and travellers, but also the remarkable combination of god of thieves, of sleep and dreams, and was permitted to travel with Charon's ferry to the underworld to accompany the souls of the dead. His characteristics were his winged shoes and hat and his herald's baton.

Poseidon, son of Rhea and brother of Zeus, ruled the sea, rivers, lakes and springs as one of the brothers of Oceanus. His companions were the Tritons and the Nereids. He demonstrated his power with the storms that whipped up the sea, and by the trident with which he could subdue it again. His dispute with Athena over the naming of the city of Athens is well known. During the argument he thrust his trident into the rock under the Acropolis, thus creating a salt-water spring, beside which Athena is said to have planted an olive tree, thus ensuring Athens' prosperity. The Greeks, being seafaring people, erected many temples and altars to Poseidon.

Zeus, father of the gods, son of Chronos and Rhea, was hidden on the island of Crete as a newborn infant, brought up by nymphs and nourished with goat's milk. He thus avoided a certain death at the hands of his father whom he later overthrew and, by using thunder and lightning bolts, established himself as the ruler of the gods and the mortals. After many long battles, he shared, with his brothers Poseidon and Hades, the power he had won over the world. He used lightning as his weapon.

The other Olympian gods are, to name but a few, Demeter, Hestia, Hephaistos, Dionysus, Persephone and Tyche, the almost unknown Greek goddess of Fortune (the equivalent of the Roman Fortuna). Today, the many legends which tell of the adventures of the gods are often recounted and read with great pleasure, as well as being represented in painting, sculpture and on stage.

Chronological table

Ancient Greece (about 900 to 500 BC)

776	First Olympic Games.
c. 750	Homer writes the *Iliad* and the *Odyssey*.
c. 600	Coinage system introduced into Greece.
c. 550	Doric architecture becomes widespread.

Classical Greece (about 500 to 320 BC)

480 to 479	The first and second military campaigns by the Persians.
450 to 429	Pericles, ruler of Athens.
447 to 432	Parthenon built.
409 to 406	Erechtheion built.
399	Socrates dies poisoned.
356 - 323	Alexander the Great.

The Hellenic Age

About 241	Attalos defeats the Galatians.
150	Setting up of the Attalos Stoa in Athens, Greece becomes a province of Rome. The modern era.
AD 395	The Goths conquer Athens.
426	Christian emperor Theodosius II closes the temples and turns them into churches.
1311	City occupied by Spaniards.
1456	Sultan Mehmet II conquers Athens, the Parthenon becomes a mosque.
1687	The Venetian Morosini conquers the Acropolis, Parthenon destroyed.
1821	Beginning of the Greek independence struggle.
1826 - 1833	Occupation of Athens by the Turks.
1834	King Otto I declares Athens capital.
1896	First Olympic Games of the modern era in Athens.
1924	Greece becomes a republic.
1936	Greece becomes a military dictatorship.
1941 - 1944	Germany occupies Greece.
1944 - 1949	Civil war, ending in the defeat of the communists.
1967	Military coup.
1975	New republic constitution.
1981	Greece joins the European Union.

Bibliography

Moritz, Karl Philipp: *Götterlehre oder Mythologische Dichtungen der Alten*. Insel-Verlag, Leipzig, 1972.

Kähler, Heinz: *Der Griechische Tempel*. Verlag Gebr. Mann, Berlin, 1964.

Time-Life Inc.: Zeitalter der Menschheit – Klassisches Griechenland. Time-Life International, Netherlands, 1966.

Droemer-Knaur: *Die Welt der Antike*; *Kulturgeschichte Griechenlands kaj Roms*. Droemersche Verlagsanstalt, Munich / Zurich, 1964.

Ling, Roger: *Kunst kaj Kultur alter Völker – Griechenland*. Karl Müller Verlag, Erlangen, 1991.

Baedeker: *Athen*. Verlag Karl Baedeker, *Ostfildern*.